W9-CGW-984

TOUGH GUYS OF HOCKEY

Paul Romanuk

Scholastic Canada Ltd

Goal scoring wasn't Bob Baun's strong point. He scored only 37 goals in his 17 seasons with the NHL, and never scored more than eight in any one season. Yet it's a goal that he's remembered for — one of the most famous in NHL history.

Bob earned his reputation as a tough, hard-nosed defenceman as a player with the Toronto Maple Leafs during the 1960s. A fixture on the blue line, along with partner Carl Brewer, Bob was known as a rock-hard bodychecker who loved to catch opponents with their guard down. His team was one of the greats in that decade, winning four Stanley Cups — three of them consecutively. But Bob earned his place in history during the 1964 Stanley Cup finals.

Game 6 of the final took place April 26, 1964. (The season ended a lot earlier back then!) The Leafs were facing elimination, trailing the Detroit Red Wings three games to two. In the third period, a Detroit player wound up and unleashed a slapshot, which rocketed into Bob's ankle. He had to be carried off the ice on a stretcher.

Still, Toronto managed to finish regulation time tied 3–3 with the Red Wings. The game went to sudden-death overtime. Meanwhile, even though he was in excruciating pain, Bob was determined to play. He ordered that his ankle be taped and frozen so that he could bear the pain and finish the game.

The overtime didn't last very long. Less than two minutes into it, Bob picked up the puck and fired a shot toward the Detroit goal. The shot deflected off Detroit defenceman Bill Gadsby and slid past Red Wings goaltender Terry Sawchuk into the net. The Leafs had won the game — and another chance at the Stanley Cup.

In the seventh, and deciding, game of the series, Toronto won 4–0 to clinch the team's third Stanley Cup in a row. Bob played in that game, too, and celebrated ecstatically with the rest of his team. Only later would he reveal that he scored that amazing game-winning goal — and went on to play another full game — while playing on a fractured leg!

All these years later, Bob is still asked about that goal more than anything else. It remains one of the most unforgettable displays of character and toughness in the history of the game.

Born: September 9, 1936, in Lanigan, Saskatchewan

Position: Defence

NHL Seasons Played: 17 (1956–57 to 1972–73)

NHL Teams: Toronto Maple Leafs, Detroit Red Wings, Oakland Seals

NHL Career Stats:

GP	G	A	PTS
964	37	187	224

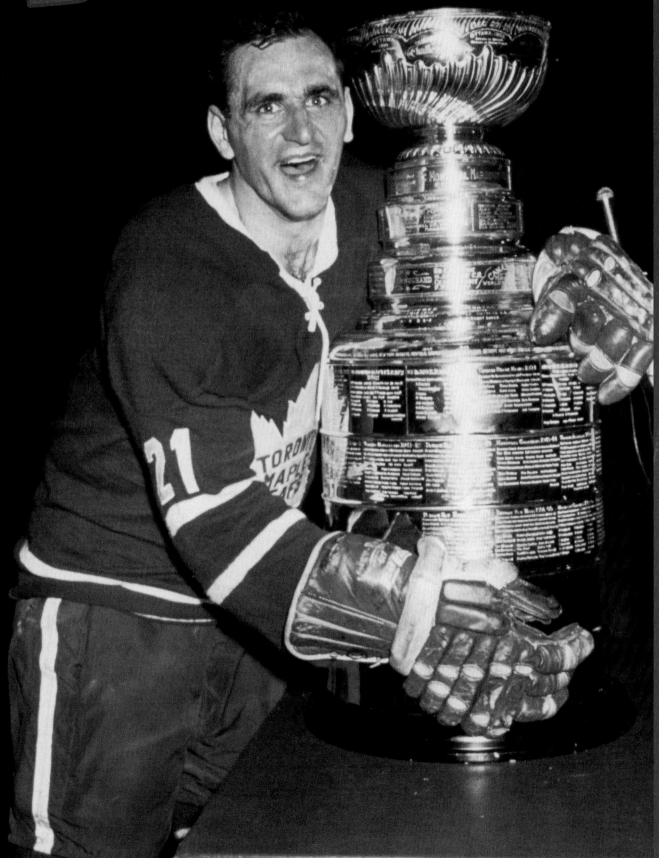

Bob BAUN

In 1978, 18-year-old Dino Ciccarelli was playing with the London Knights of the Ontario Hockey League. It was his draft year, and he was hoping to catch the eye of a few NHL scouts. But then a badly broken leg almost put an end to his career.

At first, doctors didn't give Dino much hope of ever walking properly again, let alone playing hockey. The break was so severe that a 16-inch steel rod had to be inserted into his leg to help the injury heal properly.

To his doctors' surprise, Dino's injury healed better than expected and he was able to resume his hockey career. He even made it back in time to finish the season with the Knights. But not one team was willing to take a chance on Dino on draft day.

Luckily, a few months after the draft, one very shrewd NHL general manager signed him as a free agent. Lou Nanne of the Minnesota North Stars wanted to give Dino a chance.

"I'd seen Dino play before the injury and I knew what he could do," said Nanne at the time. "I figured a kid with that kind of character at least deserved a shot at playing in the NHL, after the hard luck he had because of the leg."

Dino proved Nanne right and all of the doubters wrong.

In 1980–81, he was called up to the big club for the second half of the season, and finished strongly with 30 points in 32 games. He then turned the hockey world upside down during the playoffs. The upstart North Stars made it all the way to the Stanley Cup final, and Dino set an NHL record — 14 goals by a rookie in the post-season — a record that still stands!

By the time he called it a career after the 1998–1999 season, Dino had racked up 608 goals, putting him at number nine in all-time NHL goal-scoring.

Though he was on the small side for an NHL forward, on the ice there were few who played a more challenging game. Dino went to the net hard, and he took — and dished out — punishment that would make other players cringe.

Yet Dino is a great example of a tough player who didn't have to drop the gloves to prove it.

"I realized early in my career that I wanted to be tough, but I had to be tough without fighting. Toughness . . . is wanting to work hard," he says. "Getting up after you've been hit . . . backing up a teammate . . . standing your ground. That's toughness to me."

Born: February 8, 1960, in Sarnia, Ontario

NHL Seasons Played: 19 (1980–81 to 1998–99)

NHL Teams: Minnesota North Stars, Washington Capitals, Detroit Red Wings, Tampa Bay Lightning, Florida Panthers

Position: Right Wing

NHL Career Stats:

GP	G	A	PTS
1,232	608	592	1,200

Dino CICCARELLI

BOBBY CLARKE

Though he was a dynamic player and a natural-born leader, there were many who thought Bobby Clarke would never be able to play in the NHL. Bobby had been diagnosed with diabetes at 15 years old, and needed daily insulin injections.

On draft day, most general managers were concerned that a long NHL season would grind him into a frail athlete, unable to stand up to the physical demands of a pro hockey career. But the Philadelphia Flyers decided to take a chance. They drafted Bobby 17th overall in the 1969 Amateur Draft, and their faith was richly rewarded.

Bobby led the Flyers to the only two Stanley Cup Championships in the team's history. He played his entire 15-season career with the team, acting as captain for most of those years. He was without question the greatest player ever to wear the Flyers' colors. And today, he is the team's general manager. That's loyalty!

Bobby didn't like to bring up his illness in the early days. "When I first started in the NHL, I didn't want to be singled out or have people using it as an excuse when I had an off game. But later in my career, I grew up about it a little bit. I couldn't hide it and I didn't want to hide it. If I [could] help somebody else, especially a kid, by talking about it, then that was good."

According to Bobby, there was no secret to being a pro athlete with diabetes. He just used a lot of common sense: he watched his diet and made sure to get enough rest.

His game certainly didn't suffer. He remains the franchise leader in games played and points earned. He was named the NHL's Most Valuable Player three times, won the Selke Trophy once and was honored as Canada's Athlete of the Year in 1975.

His coach at that time, the late Fred Shero, said that he didn't think another player had ever had as much influence on a team. "As a leader, he may have made the greatest impact on the game, ever," said Shero.

His teammates couldn't help but follow his example. "He doesn't have to say anything," Paul Holmgren said at the time. "You just watch him. You see a guy like Bobby refusing to let up for even a second, trying to win all the time. How could a guy like me, or anyone else on the team, not do the same thing? I'd be embarrassed not to."

Born: August 13, 1949, in Flin Flon, Manitoba

NHL Seasons Played: 15 (1969–70 to 1983–84)

NHL Teams: Philadelphia Flyers

Position: Center

NHL Career Stats:

GP	G	A	PTS
1,144	358	852	1,210

John Cullen is a man who knows what winning is really all about.

In March 1997, John learned that a large tumor in his chest was cancerous. He underwent intense treatment, but six months after the cancer was discovered, John was given a 50:50 chance of survival. He almost died during an operation intended to fight the spread of the disease.

Then, about a year after the diagnosis, John received some wonderful news: the cancer had gone into remission.

"The day I got that news was one of the greatest days of my life," recalls John. "It had been a long, tough year but then I had a clean bill of health. I'd tried to stay positive through the whole thing."

John's teammates were almost as happy as he was when they heard the news. Although they hadn't talked about it much, John's condition had been on their minds a great deal.

"How could we not think about it all the time?" remembers one teammate. "We were wearing his number on our jerseys. Every time we looked at his empty locker, we thought about how great it would be to have him back."

Amazingly, John could now think about resuming his hockey career. He reported to the Tampa Bay Lightning's training camp in September 1998, ready to try to earn a spot on the team.

"To tell you the truth," said general manager Phil Esposito shortly afterward, "I didn't give him much of a chance to do it. I was hoping like crazy for him, though. When he made the team . . . it was one of the great stories of all time."

Unfortunately, after the first few games it became clear that John was pushing himself too hard. But he wasn't ready to quit playing yet. So, instead of retiring, he went to the minors to try and play himself back into NHL form.

"I just wouldn't be comfortable giving up two weeks into the season," he explained.

John gave it a good run in the minors with the Cleveland Lumberjacks. But in the end, he decided that his playing days were over. John took the Lightning up on their offer of a job as an assistant coach. The choice was obviously right for him.

"I knew my shot to get back to the NHL was slim," says John. "I had to make a decision. I just decided that it was time. The greatest thing was to come back, but the greatest thing of all was to be healthy."

Born: August 2, 1964, in Fort Erie, Ontario

NHL Seasons played: 10 (1988–89 to 1996–97; 1998–99)

NHL Teams: Pittsburgh Penguins, Hartford Whalers, Toronto Maple Leafs, Tampa Bay Lightning

Position: Center

NHL Career Stats:

GP	G	A	PTS
621	187	363	550

The remarkable photo opposite, taken by Frank Lennon on September 8, 1972, captures one of hockey's most memorable moments — when Paul Henderson led Canada to victory in a stunning 8-game series against the Soviet Union.

In that series, Paul played on a line with Ron Ellis and Bobby Clarke. They were hard-working players, and Team Canada was supposed to be invincible. But the Soviet team surprised Canadians with their excellence. In the first half of the series, the USSR had won two games, tied one and lost only one.

Then the Soviets won Game 5. In order to take the series, Canada would have to win each of the remaining three games.

"I remember," says Paul, "that the thought of losing the series to the Russians was just abhorrent to me. It couldn't happen. I'm not sure whether you call it toughness or character or what. I just know that our team refused to lose."

In Game 6, Paul scored the winning goal by intercepting a clearing pass at the Soviet blue line, then firing the puck past the goalie from just inside the line.

Game 7 was a little more dramatic. With the score tied 3–3, and just over two minutes left in the game, Paul took a pass just outside the Soviet blue line and charged toward the net. He made a spectacular move to beat the Soviet defenceman and blazed in on goal. As the goaltender was going down, he fired the puck over his shoulder — and into the net.

Canada had now tied the series. It would all come down to the final game.

In Game 8, Canada trailed 5–3 after two periods. They would have to score three goals in the final period to win the series. They managed to score two, but then the game was deadlocked at 5–5, with time ticking down.

In the final minute, Phil Esposito passed the puck to the front of the net to Paul. He shot. Vladislav Tretiak made the save. Paul took another shot . . .

Millions of fans at home, and thousands in the building, all gazed in awe as Paul's second shot went in. He'd scored — with 34 seconds left in the game!

Paul chalks it up to great teamwork.

"You learn some wonderful lessons in tough situations," he says. "When you try to be the hero, you never are. When you try to be a team player first, that's when you have success. I never thought about scoring the winning goal. I just thought about doing what I had to do to help us win and I ended up playing the best hockey of my life."

Born: January 28, 1943 in Kincardine, Ontario

NHL Seasons played: 13 (1962–63 to 1973–74; 1979–80)

NHL Teams: Detroit Red Wings, Toronto Maple Leafs, Atlanta Flames

Position: Left Wing

NHL Career Stats:

GP	G	A	PTS
707	236	241	477

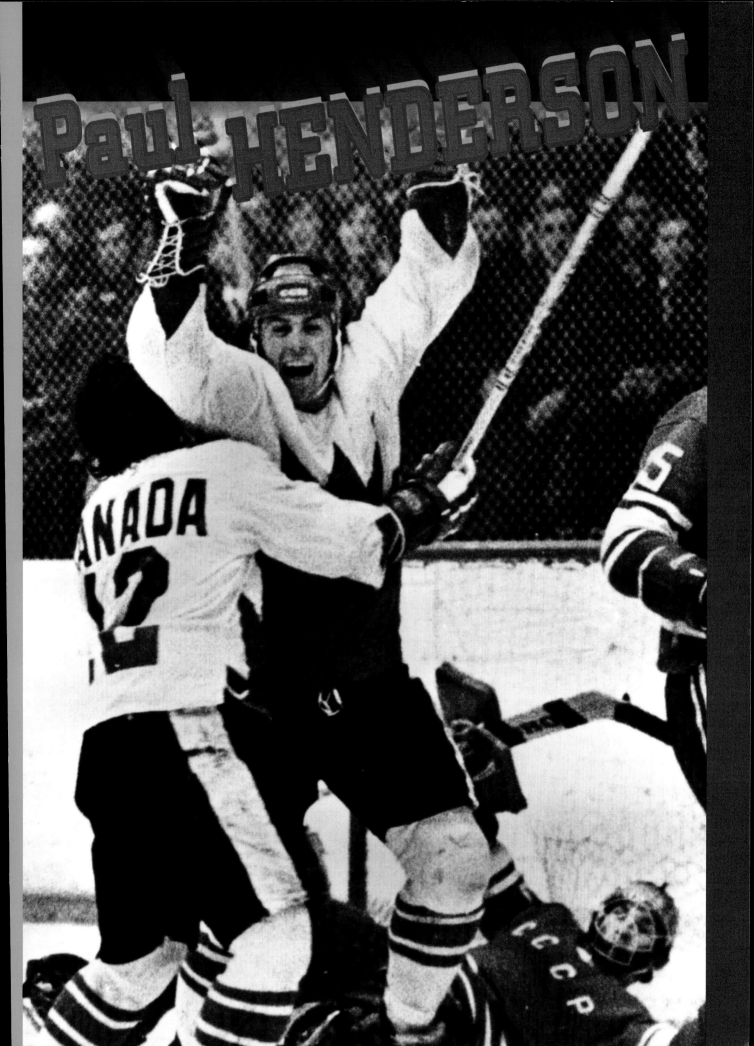

Call him "smart tough." Paul Kariya is on the small side, playing a game dominated by very large athletes — yet he finds the open spaces and succeeds. One of the ways that Paul makes room for himself is by standing his ground.

"You have to protect yourself," he says. "I think you have to make sure that guys on other teams know that you're not going to get knocked around and not do anything about it . . . Respect for your opponent has to be a two-way street."

Paul knows what he's talking about. He's been hammered by opponents a few times in his career. The most severe, and dangerous, hit was a cross-check to the jaw during the 1997–98 season. Paul missed the last 28 games of the season recovering from it.

Paul was a brilliant player before he ever reached the NHL. In his final season of college hockey, he led the Maine Black Bears to their first ever NCAA championship. He also won the 1993 Hobey Baker Award as the top player in US college hockey. He was drafted in the first round by the Mighty Ducks of Anaheim. But rather than join them right away, he first played for Canada's national team, helping to lead them to a silver-medal finish at the 1994 Olympics.

Throughout his dazzling career, Paul has remained down to earth. Paul's former coach in Anaheim, Ron Wilson, tells a story about the time he and the team's general manager traveled to Paul's home for dinner and some contract discussions.

"We went there to offer this 18-year-old kid millions of dollars," recalls Wilson. "After it's over, Paul's mother asks Paul to clear away the dishes from the table. Away he went, no complaints, no attitude, nothing."

The way Paul conducts himself off the ice earns him respect from his team's management and the fans. And on the ice, he has the complete respect of the players. He is an amazing skater, a slick passer and one of the most intelligent players ever to lace on a pair of skates.

"He's just plain fun to watch," says Philadelphia star Eric Lindros.

Paul's friend and teammate Teemu Selanne agrees. "When you watch another player make a great play, you usually say 'I could do that,' but with Paul sometimes I just go 'wow.' He's exciting to watch and to play with."

Born: October 16, 1974, in Vancouver, British Columbia

Anaheim's 1st pick (4th overall) — 1993 NHL Entry Draft

First NHL Team and Season: Mighty Ducks of Anaheim (1994–95)

Position: Left Wing

Shoots: Left

Height: 1.80 m (5'11")

Weight: 82 kg (180 lbs.)

Not only did Mario Lemieux make an incredible comeback, but he came back to dominate like never before.

In the 1992–93 season, Mario was at the top of his game. The Pittsburgh Penguins were coming off back-to-back Stanley Cup Championships and were favoured to win another. Mario was on his way to another scoring title.

But in January 1993, he was diagnosed with Hodgkin's disease. The good news was that Hodgkin's is a type of cancer that has a good rate of recovery if detected early. In Mario's case they had caught it at an early stage.

He was treated with radiation therapy, which brings with it a side effect of extreme fatigue.

"You feel like you've been run over," Mario explained at the time. "It really takes a lot out of you."

Still, after taking a month off for the treatments, Mario wanted to return to the ice. Amazingly, he went on to win his fourth NHL scoring title as well the Hart Trophy for Most Valuable Player. It was only later that he would admit to how unwell he had felt that year.

The following season, Mario was hobbled by back problems. He was also still feeling the effects of radiation therapy from the year before, and he conceded that perhaps he hadn't allowed his body enough time to recover. Mario only played 22 games that season, then decided to take the entire 1994–95 season off to allow his injuries to heal. Many felt that his career was finished.

But he had another surprise to spring on the sports world. He returned the following year and was spectacular. He won another scoring title, another Hart Trophy and the respect and admiration of players and fans everywhere.

"It was like a second chance for me," says Mario. "I enjoyed every moment out there with my teammates . . . I didn't take it for granted."

"I think we were all amazed at the things Mario was doing after not playing for so long," says Pittsburgh GM Craig Patrick. "It was as though he hadn't missed a game, never mind an entire season."

After his comeback year, Mario played one more season — winning his sixth scoring title — and then retired for good.

He has since gone on to become the owner of the Pittsburgh Penguins, a move which came as a surprise to some. But when it comes to Mario, could anything be that much of a surprise?

Born: October 5, 1965, in Montreal, Quebec

NHL Seasons Played: 12 (1984–85 to 1993–94; 1995-96 to 1996–97)

NHL Teams: Pittsburgh Penguins

Position: Center

NHL Career Stats:

GP	G	A	PTS
745	613	881	1,494

GRANT MARSHALL

"For dedication, perseverance, determination . . . I don't think that Grant's story could ever be topped." So says Grant Marshall's old coach, Brian Kilrea.

On December 4, 1990, Grant's junior team, the Ottawa 67's, were playing the Sudbury Wolves. Grant was heading toward the boards to play the puck when he was hit from behind. He crashed into the boards headfirst.

"I was lying there, conscious, and realized that I couldn't move," says Grant. "I couldn't move my arms, legs or anything for two or three minutes. I was terrified. I thought my life was finished.

"I remember thinking, when the injury first happened, that I just wanted to be a normal kid . . . to have a normal life."

Tests were run and the good news was that Grant would eventually be fine. He was fitted with a halo device to hold his head and spine in place so the injury could properly heal. And sure enough, Grant was back on his skates by March 1991 — and itching to get into a game with his team. He was determined to make it back into the lineup before the season was over.

"I begged the coach to let me back into a game," remembers Grant. "I wouldn't take no for an answer."

On April 18, he was set to come back. Ottawa was facing elimination against the Oshawa Generals in a playoff game. To the astonishment of the crowd, on his very first shift of the game, Grant landed a solid hit on a big, hulking forward . . . named Eric Lindros.

Grant smiles when he's reminded of the game. "I figured I might as well try things out and go after the biggest guy. I knew I was back."

The following season Grant starred with Ottawa, picking up 134 points. His NHL career began after he was drafted in the first round in 1992, by the Toronto Maple Leafs. He moved on to the Dallas Stars in 1994, and took part in that team's 1999 Stanley Cup championship.

"After we won the Cup," recalls Grant, "I was a little emotional. I realized how special my life had been to that point . . . It made me realize how lucky I was. I was very happy and grateful."

For Grant, being tough is all about overcoming fear and having self-respect. It's also about playing with confidence.

"Playing the game the way you can as hard as you can . . . so that your teammates and opponents respect you. That defines a tough player."

Born: June 9, 1973, in Mississauga, Ontario

Toronto's 2nd pick (23rd overall) — 1992 NHL Entry Draft

First NHL Team and Season: Dallas Stars, 1994–95

Position: Right Wing

Shoots: Right

Height: 1.85 m (6' 1")

Weight: 88 kg (193 lbs.)

GRANT MARSHALL

Any hockey player or coach has had to fight through some adversity. But in Ted Nolan's case, there have been a few extra obstacles.

Ted, an Ojibway band member, grew up on the Garden River Reserve in northern Ontario. When he left at the age of 16 to pursue his dream of a hockey career, it was the first time he had ever been away from home.

"You leave home to play hockey as a kid in Canada and that's pretty typical," says Ted, "but for a Native kid it's a real culture shock. It's a very different way of life away from the reservation. It's a different culture and a different approach to many everyday things."

At times, Ted had to endure severe racial prejudice. Then in 1981, as his career in the NHL was just beginning, he received awful news: his mother had been killed by a drunk driver.

"The toughest part was coming home after the accident and having to decide whether or not to leave my family again," remembers Ted. "I almost didn't go back to my hockey career. I had to make a man's decision while I was still a kid, and that was difficult."

But Ted did go back, and is happy he did. He played in 78 NHL games — mostly with the Detroit Red Wings — before an injury forced him to retire in 1986. He went on to work as an assistant coach with the Hartford Whalers, and then became Head Coach for the Buffalo Sabres in July 1995.

It was as a coach that Ted really came into his own. In 1996–97, his second season with the Sabres, Ted pushed his club to be the best it could be. Buffalo went from being a fifth-place to a first-place team. What the Sabres lacked in raw skill, they made up for with effort and a driving spirit. Buffalo earned a reputation as a tough opponent, and Ted won respect as a coach who could motivate his players and get the best out of them.

In recognition of his amazing achievements, Ted was presented with the 1997 Jack Adams Award for NHL Coach of the Year. It was a very proud moment for him.

With his coaching career on hold for the time being, Ted is now very busy working with First Nation kids, for whom he is an inspiring role model.

"I always said to myself that if I ever made it to the NHL, even just for one game, than I would come back and tell other kids that they could overcome obstacles and make it too."

Born: April 7, 1958, in Sault Ste. Marie, Ontario

NHL Seasons Coached: 2 (1995–96 to 1996–97)

NHL Teams Coached: Buffalo Sabres

NHL Coaching Stats (to date):

GC	W	L	T	W%
164	73	72	19	.503

The youngest of twelve children, Willie O'Ree was born in Fredericton, New Brunswick, in 1935. He played junior hockey in Kitchener, Ontario, and eventually ended up with a minor pro team in Quebec City before getting his big break in the NHL in January 1958. At the same time he made history — becoming the NHL's first Black player.

Willie played two seasons with the Boston Bruins, and continued to play in the minor leagues until 1978–79. Though his NHL career may have been brief, it was significant, marking a real shift toward racial equality in sports.

He was often called "the Jackie Robinson of hockey," after the first Black major-league baseball player. Yet Willie didn't feel that racism was as big an issue for him.

"I'm aware of being the first [Black player], and the responsibilities," he said in an interview at the time. "But there never has been the discrimination in this game that there was in baseball, and I didn't face any of the very real problems that Robinson had to face."

Still, Willie was a racial pioneer of sorts, and he had to endure some of the difficulties that come with that territory.

"I heard the names; I had heard them growing up," he said after he had retired from the game. "I heard it from the opposition and from some fans."

Though Willie fought a lot, he never dropped the gloves in response to racial taunts.

"I wanted to represent myself and the team I played for to the best of my ability," he says. "I couldn't have done that if I was fighting all the time." It helped that Willie's teammates, and most Boston fans, were his biggest supporters. They treated him just like any other player on the team.

One of Willie's fondest memories is of the time he scored his first NHL goal.

"It was New Year's Day, 1961, in Boston," he remembers. "It was a game-winner against the Montreal Canadiens."

After the goal was scored the Boston fans gave Willie a standing ovation.

"I never thought about being the first Black NHL player," recalls Willie all these years later. "I was just happy to be in the NHL. I was excited because we won the game. I didn't really stop and think about it, until later, that I had broken the color barrier."

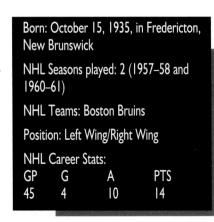

Born: October 15, 1935, in Fredericton, New Brunswick

NHL Seasons played: 2 (1957–58 and 1960–61)

NHL Teams: Boston Bruins

Position: Left Wing/Right Wing

NHL Career Stats:

GP	G	A	PTS
45	4	10	14

Willie O'REE

Let's face it: anyone who makes a living stopping frozen pucks is tough. But Jacques Plante stands out from the crowd because he was an innovator. His decision to stand up to critics literally changed the face of goaltending.

It's hard to believe now, but there was a time when goalies did not wear masks! They were used only when a player had an injured nose to protect, and there was never any thought that they should be adopted as part of goalies' regular equipment. It wasn't until the early 1970s, after Jacques had influenced the game, that masks became commonplace.

Jacques started wearing one back in the late 1950s, during practices with the Montreal Canadiens, as protection after a sinus operation. Practice was one thing, but Montreal management were against Jacques using the mask in a game. They thought it displayed a weakness and fear of the puck on his part.

Then, on November 1, 1959, Jacques was hit in the face during a game. It was a severe cut, and he had to leave the ice to be stitched up. There were no backup goalies back then, so play was halted while Jacques was being tended to.

It was then that Jacques put his foot down. He steadfastly refused to re-enter the game unless he could wear his mask — which he designed himself — during play.

Montreal's coach, the legendary Toe Blake, wasn't happy with his goaltender's demand. But he was less happy about having to play the rest of the game without Plante. So the mask stayed. And Jacques' play was sensational: the Canadiens went on to win their game against the Rangers, and started an 18-game undefeated streak! From then on, Jacques' mask was as much a part of his game as his stick.

Though it took a long time for the hockey establishment to come around, eventually all goaltenders adopted the mask — and spared themselves a lot of injury.

Jacques is hailed as one of the greatest players ever. His name appears on the Vezina Trophy a record seven times. He won the Hart Trophy as the NHL's Most Valuable Player in 1962. His career-wins total is the second-highest of all time.

For his innovation, but first and foremost because of his great goaltending, Jacques was inducted into the Hockey Hall of Fame in 1978.

Born: January 17, 1929, in Shawinigan Falls, Quebec

Died: February 27, 1986

NHL Seasons played: 18 (1952–53 to 1964–65; 1968–69 to 1972–73)

NHL Teams: Montreal Canadiens, New York Rangers, St. Louis Blues, Toronto Maple Leafs, Boston Bruins

Position: Goaltender

NHL Career Stats:

GP	GA	SO	GAA
837	1,965	82	2.38

Manon Rhéaume started her hockey career the way most Canadian kids do — playing shinny and taking shots with her brothers. She went on to become a trailblazer: the first woman ever to play pro hockey, and the first to play in an NHL game.

Manon showed great talent at a young age, with reflexes and an eye for the puck that made her tough to beat. At only 11 years old, she was the first girl ever to play in the Quebec International Pee-Wee Hockey Tournament, one of the most prestigious tournaments in the world for young players.

In her teens, Manon continued to play on boys' teams, and also traveled from her home in Quebec City to Montreal — a couple of hours' drive each way — to play for a women's team.

"It was never easy," Manon would say later. "But I always wanted to play hockey. I love the game and have always had a great desire to play it."

At the age of 19, she stepped onto the ice to play for the Trois-Rivières Draveurs of the Quebec Major Junior Hockey League.

Then in 1992, at 20 years old, she was invited to training camp for the Tampa Bay Lightning. On September 23, Manon played in an exhibition game against the St. Louis Blues. She played one period, facing seven shots and giving up two goals. But more importantly, Manon had made hockey history!

Though she didn't make the Lightning, she did earn a spot with their minor league team in Atlanta. She became the first woman to sign a professional hockey contract, and on December 3, 1992, was the first to play in a regular-season game. Manon has continued her professional career in the minors with various teams.

In addition to her pro hockey career, Manon has been a major force on Canada's National Women's Hockey Team. She and her team won gold at the World Championships in 1992 and 1994 and she was named to the tournament all-star team both years. She helped Canada to a silver-medal finish at the 1998 Olympics, the first year women's hockey was a part of the games. She has also made waves in professional roller hockey.

Manon took some time off after giving birth to a boy in May of 1999. But it won't slow her down.

"I'm on a three-year program," she says. "I'll build myself back into shape and get back at it. It will be intense and hard work, but I'll be there."

Born: February 24, 1972, in Lac Beauport, Quebec

Signed as a free agent by the Atlanta Knights (IHL) in 1992

Position: Goaltender

Catches: Left

Height: 1.68 m (5'6")

Weight: 59 kg (130 lbs.)

Manon RHÉAUME

On any given NHL team there are players from all over the world, but it hasn't always been that way. As recently as the 1980s, almost all of the players in the league were born and trained in Canada.

The man who blazed the trail for international players to come to the NHL was a tough and determined Swedish defenceman named Borje Salming.

Borje was already a hockey hero in Sweden when he was discovered by a Toronto Maple Leafs scout in the early 1970s. He had dazzling puck-handling and skating skills, and was a smart defensive player.

What Borje would have to prove to Canadian fans and players was that he could take the physical style of play in the NHL. The league was considered to be much tougher, physically, than any other in the world. Borje was not readily accepted by North Americans. Rarely in the history of the NHL has a player taken so much physical and verbal abuse. "Chicken Swede" and "coward" were a couple of the tamer barbs that Borje would hear from fans and opponents.

He was run into the boards, slashed and otherwise challenged by the enforcers on other teams. But Borje stood his ground, proving himself to be as tough as any other player. He paid no mind to the abuse and instead focused on helping his team.

The turning point for Borje was during a 1976 Stanley Cup playoff game against the Philadelphia Flyers — known at the time as the "Broad Street Bullies" for their extremely aggressive style of play. Though the game was filled with fights, Borje ignored them and concentrated on playing hockey. He was cut on the face and had to have eight stitches, but he played on.

Then, when Borje scored a goal that put the Leafs in front in the third period, the building erupted with one of the loudest and longest standing ovations ever heard at the old Maple Leaf Gardens. Through his great and courageous play, Borje had finally earned the respect of opponents and fans around the league.

Borje was the first European player to appear in 1,000 NHL games and, in 1996, became the first Swedish-born player ever inducted into the Hockey Hall of Fame. And thanks to him, toughness is now measured by a player's personality, not his nationality.

Born: April 17, 1951, in Kiruna, Sweden

NHL Seasons played: 17 (1973–74 to 1989–90)

NHL Teams: Toronto Maple Leafs, Detroit Red Wings

Position: Defence

NHL Career Stats:

GP	G	A	PTS
1,148	150	637	787

Borje Salming

The same "go hard or go home" attitude that got him into the NHL all those years ago has remained with Brian Skrudland through his entire career.

"Both of my parents were hard-working people," says Brian. "They taught me a lot . . . Work ethic has been a major part of my success."

After a solid but unspectacular junior career with the Saskatoon Blades of the Western Hockey League, no team saw fit to draft him. Happily, the Montreal Canadiens decided that any kid who worked as hard as Brian deserved a chance. He was signed as a free agent in September 1993 and invited to training camp. Brian was assigned to the minors, where he played for the next two seasons. But he never stopped believing that he'd make it to the big club.

Of course, he was right: he finally got his chance to play on the team in the 1985–86 season. And what a season it was. Led by a young goaltender named Patrick Roy, the Canadiens won the Stanley Cup.

"It was amazing," recalls Brian. "Not only did I make it to the NHL but I was a part of a Stanley Cup in my first season. I couldn't believe it."

After that exciting year, it would be 13 seasons before Brian would sip champagne from the Cup again.

"I think that when you're a young guy and you win it, you figure that it will happen again. You have lots of time. But then the years go by and all of a sudden you realize just how tough it is to win a Stanley Cup. It's just tough to stay in the league, period. It's hard work."

During those long years, Brian missed over 200 games with an astounding list of injuries. But in each case, he was determined to work hard and earn his way back into the lineup. And he furthered his reputation as a player who would never quit on a team. The payoff came when, as a veteran player, he helped the Dallas Stars to win the 1999 Stanley Cup Championship.

"Toughness to me is when someone tells you 'you can't' or 'you're not capable' and you go out there and respond to that with a belief in yourself and your own ability.

"We have a saying on our fridge at home, and it says: 'The man who wins is the man who thinks he can.' That says it all to me."

Born: July 31, 1963, in Peace River, Alberta

Signed as a free agent by Montreal in 1983

First NHL Team and Season: Montreal Canadiens, 1985–86

Position: Center

Shoots: Left

Height: 1.83 m (6')

Weight: 89 kg (195 lbs.)

Brian SKRUDLAND

It's more like a scene from a James Bond movie than a hockey story: a car races across the countryside, one step ahead of the secret police, carrying its passengers over the border to freedom. But that is how Peter Stastny's dream of an NHL career started to come true.

Peter was one of the greatest players in the world back in the mid-1970s. But playing hockey anywhere other than his home country, then-communist Czechoslovakia, was something he could only dream about.

At that time, players from communist nations were not allowed to move to another country to play professional sports. If they were caught trying to flee, their careers would be ruined. While many athletes were happy to stay in their home countries, Peter wanted more.

It was while playing for the Czech national team that he and his brothers, Marian and Anton, caught the attention of North American fans and NHL teams. Peter and Marian played in the 1976 Canada Cup with a powerful Czechoslovakian team that made it all the way to the final, before losing to Canada. All three also played in the 1980 Olympics, but it was Peter who excelled. He finished second in tournament scoring with 14 points in 7 games.

Shortly after the Olympics, Peter and Anton huddled in a car with Quebec Nordiques' owner Marcel Aubut, speeding across the Austrian countryside toward the airport in Vienna. Aubut had brought a six-year contract for each brother and made secret arrangements for their escape.

"It was pretty scary," Aubut would later say. "I don't think there is any doubt that we would have been in very big trouble if we had been caught. At the time we felt our lives were in danger."

Just as scary for Peter must have been leaving the life he was familiar with — his friends, teammates and much of his family — to take a chance on a career in the NHL. But it was a risk worth taking. Peter exploded into the league, tallying 109 points in his first season, and was named Rookie of the Year. He played his heart out for the Nordiques for 10 seasons, before finishing his luminous career with stints in New Jersey and St. Louis. The icing on the cake came in 1998, when Peter was inducted into the Hockey Hall of Fame.

"When I was a boy I had many dreams," Peter said later, "but I never dreamed that I would be in the Hall of Fame one day. It's a big honor."

Born: September 18, 1956, in Bratislava, Czechoslovakia

NHL Seasons Played: 15 (1980–81 to 1994–95)

NHL Teams: Quebec Nordiques, New Jersey Devils, St. Louis Blues

Position: Center

NHL Career Stats:

GP	G	A	PTS
977	450	789	1,239

Peter STASTNY

In memory of my dad, a tough guy with a heart of gold.

Photo credits

Bob Baun, Willie O'Ree, Jacques Plante: Imperial Oil–Turofsky/Hockey Hall of Fame;
Dino Ciccarelli, Peter Stastny: Frank Howard/Protography;
John Cullen: Jon Hayt/Bruce Bennett Studios;
Bobby Clarke, Paul Kariya, Ted Nolan, Borje Salming, Brian Skrudland: Bruce Bennett/Bruce Bennett Studios;
Theoren Fleury (cover): John Giamundo/Bruce Bennett Studios;
Paul Henderson: CP Photo Archive (Frank Lennon);
Mario Lemieux: Paul Angers/Bruce Bennett Studios;
Grant Marshall: Dave Sandford/Hockey Hall of Fame;
Manon Rhéaume: Eileen Connors/Bruce Bennett Studios.

Abbreviations used in this book: A = Assists; G = Goals; GA = Goals Against;
GAA = Goals Against Average; GC = Games Coached; GP = Games Played;
L = Losses; PTS = Points; SO = Shutouts; T = Ties;
W = Wins; W% = Win Percentage.

Canadian Cataloguing in Publication Data

Romanuk, Paul
Tough guys of hockey: sixteen players who beat the odds

ISBN 0-590-24856-1

1. Hockey players — Biography — Juvenile literature. 2. National Hockey League
— Biography — Juvenile literature. 3. Hockey — Juvenile literature. I. Title.

GV848.5.A1R66 2000   j796.962'092'2   C99-932842-5

Copyright © 2000 by Scholastic Canada Ltd. All rights reserved.
No part of this publication may be reproduced or stored in a retrieval system, or transmitted in any form or by
any means, electronic, mechanical, recording, or otherwise, without written permission of the publisher,
Scholastic Canada Ltd., 175 Hillmount Road, Markham, Ontario, Canada L6C 1Z7.
In the case of photocopying or other reprographic copying, a licence must be obtained from
CANCOPY (Canadian Copyright Licensing Agency), 1 Yonge Street, Suite 1900, Toronto, Ontario, M5E 1E5.

6 5 4 3 2 1   Printed in Canada   0 1 2 3 4/0